SYMBOLS

& Their Meaning

by Rolf Myller

Atheneum 1978 New York

LIBRARY OF CONGRESS CATALOGING IN PUBLICATION DATA

Myller, Rolf.   Symbols.

SUMMARY: Brief text and illustrations
examine the use of symbols for quick and simple
communications.
1. Signs and symbols—Juvenile literature.
[1. Signs and symbols]   I. Title.
AZ108.M9   001.56   77-17015
ISBN 0-689-30638-5

Published simultaneously in Canada by
McClelland & Stewart, Ltd.
Manufactured in the United States of America by
The Book Press, Brattleboro, Vermont
First Edition

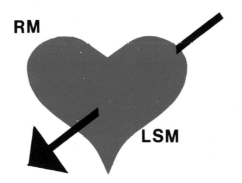

It has been said that one picture is worth a thousand words. This makes the picture, a symbol of a complicated thought, a shortcut in communication. However, even the most basic of the thousand words is itself a symbol, for every word we use is a concept so complex that it usually requires several lines of dictionary explanation.

For anything to be a symbol, at least two people must understand and accept its meaning.

A burp, for instance, considered rude by us, becomes a symbol of appreciation for a well-cooked meal in certain far-off places. In the right situation then, a well-timed burp becomes a symbol of and for good taste.

This book is about some of the symbols we use and their meanings.

sym•bol (sim'b'l) n. [< Fr.&L.: Fr. *symbole* < L. *symbolus,* *symbolum* < Gr. *symbolon,* token, pledge, sign by which one infers a thing *symballein,* to throw together, compare < *syn-,* together + *ballein,* to throw] 1. something that stands for or represents another thing; esp., an object used to represent something abstract; emblem (the dove is a symbol of peace) 2. a written or printed mark, letter, abbreviation, etc. standing for an object, quality, process, quantity, etc. as in music, mathematics, or chemistry* *Webster's New World Dictionary,* Second College Edition Copyright © 1976 by William Collins + World Publishing Co., Inc.

Pointing is a means of communication that a child learns before he is able to understand or use words. When a mother wants to identify something specific for a child, she points to it; soon when the child wants something, he also points. Pointing, in a way, becomes a shortcut, or a symbol, for words and, of course, direction.

With civilizations, as with children, pointing probably was among the first symbols used. Arrows point; there is never any question as to where an arrow points. Originally, primitive man shot the arrow at a target, and even though the arrow's flight involves sophisticated aerodynamic principles, the directional action is plain common sense, and the shape of the arrow to this day has remained a symbol for direction that everybody understands.

The Zulus say **UBUTHI** or **ISIHLUNGU.**

In Swahili they say **SUMU.** In Tagalog, **LASON.**

In Samoa they say **VAI'O'ONA,**
and in Italian it's **VELENO.**

In Cantonese they say **DUHK-YEUHK.**

In Hungarian **MÉREG,** and it's **TRUCIZNA** in Polish.

The Welsh say **GWENWYN,** the Irish say **NIMH,**
and the Turks call it **ZEHIR.**

The word is **OTROV** in Croatian, and **MYRKKY** in Finnish,
while in Malay it is called **RACHUN.**

The Dakota Indians say **PEZUTASICA,** and the Hawaiians
use **HE MEA MAKE KE AI IA A INU PAHA** or **'APU KŌHE OHEO** for short.

Most of us don't know what these words mean. But when a skull with crossbones is used on a bottle, it is immediately recognized and respected by everyone. Even to young children, the skull with crossbones means danger, death and **POISON.**

Messages conveying warnings of danger have a priority in the world of symbols, for often there is no time to lose with complicated instructions, and no room for misunderstanding.

Diagonal or crossed lines are the accepted short cut for the words NO and DON'T.

Though the image of a skull implies death, even when shown by itself, the crossed bones behind it use the "X" shape to reinforce the warning. "X" signs are used at railroad crossings, as warnings where the ice is too thin to walk on safely, and to indicate where there is high voltage that can electrocute whoever touches it.

Traffic signs are international and require no words of explanation. These graphic signs are simple and direct. They can be understood at a glance, for that is all a driver has time for when he is traveling at high speeds. The message must be communicated to him instantly, and the images on the signs become symbols for information that automatically registers in his mind.

Color is significant in signage:

RED indicates stop, or a prohibition.
GREEN shows movement permitted, or gives directional guidance.
BLUE is for signs leading to motorist services.
YELLOW indicates a general warning.
BLACK on white are regulatory signs, such as those for speed indications.
ORANGE conveys construction and maintenance warnings.
BROWN is for public recreation and scenic guidance.

Shapes have meanings:

DIAMOND-SHAPED SIGNS signify a warning.
RECTANGULAR SIGNS with the longer dimension vertical provide a traffic regula-
    tion.
RECTANGULAR SIGNS with the longer dimension horizontal contain guidance in-
    formation.
AN OCTAGON means STOP.
AN INVERTED TRIANGLE means YIELD.
A PENNANT means no passing.
A PENTAGON shows that there is a school.

YIELD

SPEED LIMIT 50

NO RIGHT TURN

STOP

NO BICYCLES

DO NOT ENTER

When lines are crossed in a different manner, the result is a simple cross, which is best known as the symbol for Christianity, a form that commemorates the crucifixion of Jesus Christ.

Originally the Christians used the Greek letter X or chi as their symbol, which was the first letter of ΧΡΙΣΤΟΣ, the Greek word for Christ. In fact, sometimes the first two letters were used—XP, or chi-rho—woven into a variety of patterns.

Crosses in many variations are worn for both religious and decorative purposes: they are carried in processions; they are made part of the ceremonial dress of the clerics; they form the basic design in flags and banners; they are part of the architecture of buildings; and they are used to mark the graves of the faithful Christians.

BYZANTINE CONSECRATION CROSS

CROSS PATTY OR FORMY (THE IRON CROSS)

RUSSIAN CROSS

GREEK CROSS

X-SHAPED CROSS OR SALTIRE

CHI-RHO

CROSS OF LORRAINE

PAPAL CROSS

MALTESE CROSS

LATIN OR LONG CROSS

The Ankh is a variation of the cross that was used by the ancient Egyptians. It is also known as the *crux ansata,* and it symbolizes Life to Come. The sign is formed by adding a circle, the Egyptian symbol for eternity, to the top of the T or tau, their symbol for life.

Variations of the Ankh are found in ancient cultures as diverse as those of the Aztecs and the Phoenicians. Its significance appears to have been consistently of a mystical or religious nature; for example, when the sign appears with the circle below the cross, it has been known to represent the concept of Goodness.

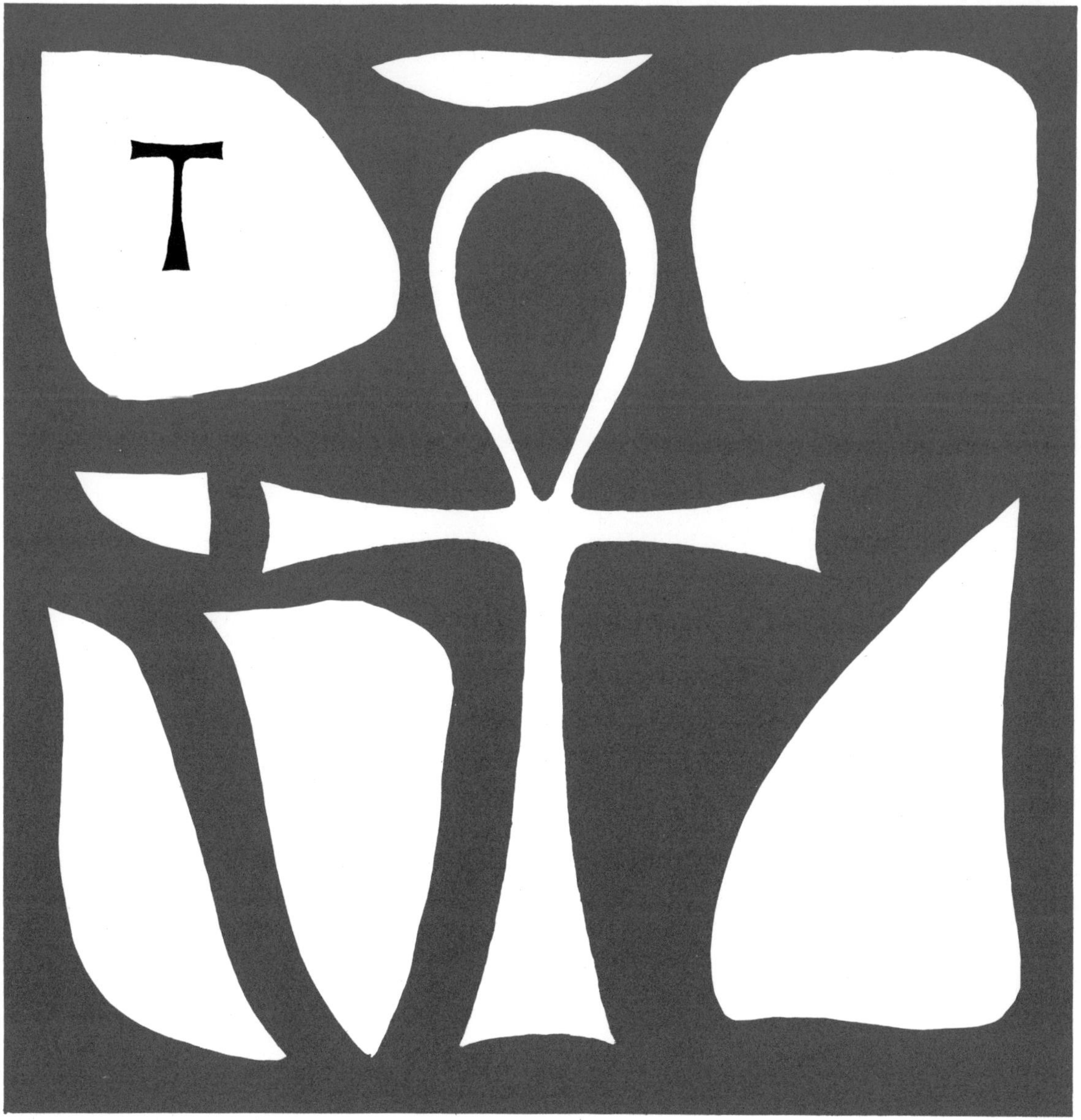
T

We think of the swastika as a symbol of terror, vicious mass murder and senseless destruction. It was adopted by the German Nazis, who used the sign on their flags, their armbands, on belt buckles, and wherever else they wanted an insignia. It will be long before our instinct will allow us to see this powerful design without associations of horror.

But it was not always so; the Swastika or Fylfot Cross is one of the most common variations of the non-Christian cross. It appears in many ancient cultures. It was used by the Hindus and the Buddhists in India, by the early Babylonians, Persians, and Assyrians.

When the Chinese used it in blue, it symbolized Infinite Celestial Virtue, and in yellow it meant Infinite Prosperity. To some tribes of the North American Indians, it represented the four directions, and to other tribes it stood for the four seasons. The Greeks liked the design and used it simply for decoration.

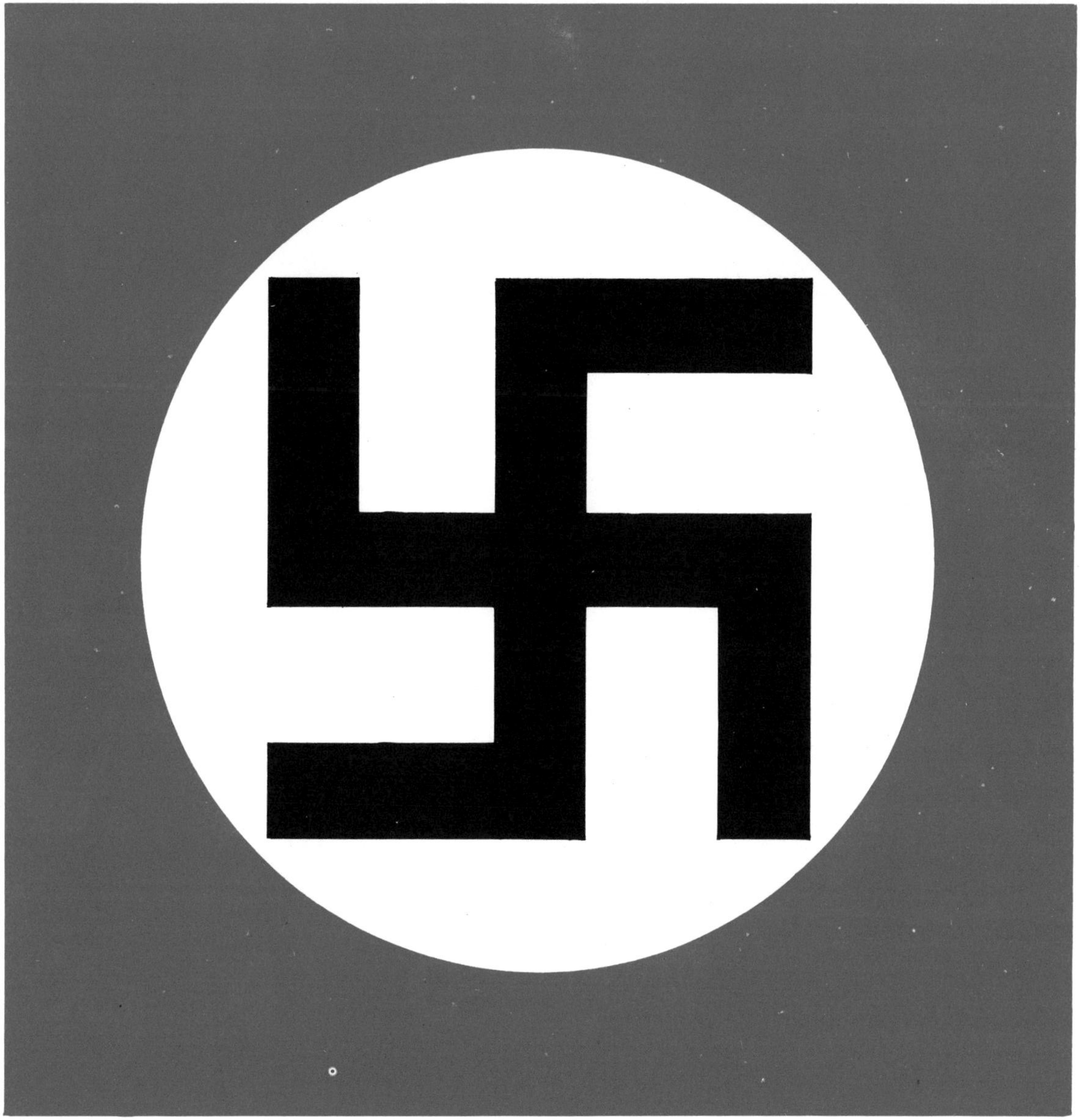

The RED cross on a white background symbolizes mercy and aid to the sick and wounded. Hospitals, ambulances and even first aid kits are identified with a red cross.

There is an international understanding that in times of war, any place that is marked with the red cross is neutral territory, and the combatants will usually respect this agreement.

However, color is important to symbolism.
When the red cross is reversed
and becomes a WHITE cross against a red background,
it is the emblem and flag of Switzerland.

Flags are symbols.

"I pledge allegiance to the flag of the United States of America and to the Republic for which it stands . . ." clearly indicates that the American flag is more than just a colorful design that makes parades more festive. The well-known pledge goes so far as to say that the flag is a symbol for a great concept.

Similarly, the flags of other countries symbolize entire cultures and national heritages. In most countries the flags are almost worshipped: they are saluted and handled with honor and respect; soldiers have gone into battle throughout history, and millions have died for the ideals that their flags represented to them.

The white flag is the international symbol for surrender. Even a white handkerchief or an undershirt that is white will communicate the idea. Whoever waves the white cloth is saying without the use of words: "I give up!"

"Hands up!" means the same thing. Whether in time of war or in the case of a criminal who comes out of hiding with his hands up, the message is surrender. The historical background of this gesture is obvious, for anyone with his hands raised does not hold weapons.

The dove is an ancient symbol for peace. The hawk on the other hand is a predatory bird that is associated with aggressiveness.

During the war in Vietnam, the label given to the group of people who believed that the solution to wars could be found through discussion was "doves," while "hawks" were those who believed that peace should be achieved through fighting.

The symbol adopted by the "doves" to express their ideal of peace is a young design, one that has evolved in the age of the jet plane. The symbol also stands for nuclear disarmament, and its message is understood around the world.

The "Shield of David" is a six-pointed star formed by two equilateral triangles that have the same center and are placed in opposite directions.

The star is the official emblem of Judaism and the main theme in the design of the flag of Israel.

In spite of the name "Shield of David," or magen david, there is little in history that suggests that it was used for anything but decorative purposes by both Jews and non-Jews in biblical times. One of the earliest Jewish uses appears in a synagogue in Capernaum, built some twenty-two centuries ago; there, in fact, the symbol appears side by side with the swastika and other designs.

In 1354 the ruler of the city of Prague granted the Jewish community there the priviledge of having its own flag, with the star, which was then believed to have been the coat of arms that King David wore on his shield to battle. From that time on the six-pointed star gradually became the accepted symbol of Judaism.

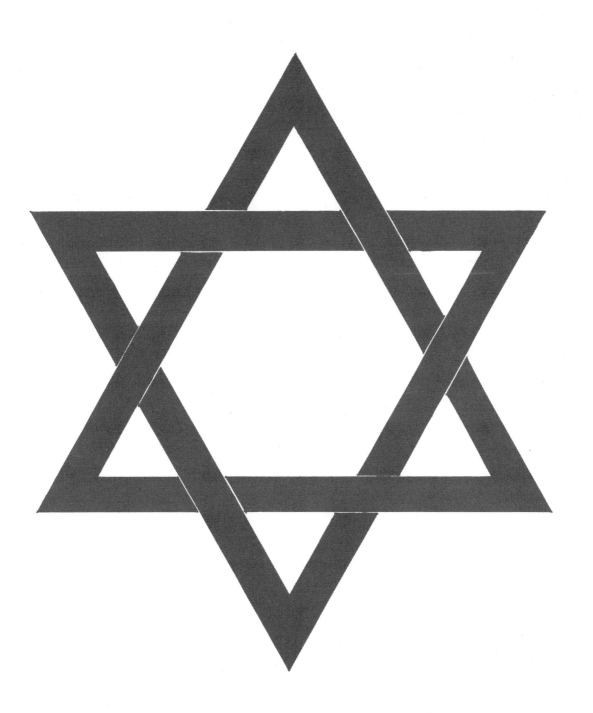

The Yin and Yan is an old Chinese symbol that demonstrates the perfection of Nature, of God and of the entire universe.

The design shows that unity is made of opposites—a balance that may stand for good and evil, hot and cold, earth and air, light and dark, passive and active, sun and moon, and so on.

Yin and Yan can also stand for man and woman. There are two separate, dynamic equals, which work in complimentary contrast. Without either, the other would be meaningless, but together, they form a powerful unity.

More specific than the Yin and Yan are the biological symbols for male and female.

Originally, the signs were used by scientists to label and distinguish the sex of living things, whether bird or bug or plant or whale.

More recently, however, the symbols have been adopted by various groups and organizations to express their strong identification with one sex or another.

Love!

Need more be said?

There is a whole range of body language with which people communicate wordlessly.

Who does not know the meaning of a friendly smile, a nod of approval, an angry frown or a "don't-know" shrug. A different type shrug may be saying "I don't care" or "who knows?" The shaking of the head vertically may mean an affirmative, while if the head moves from side to side the answer may be no. An extended hand is a sign of friendship, open arms a welcome, and a raised palm may command a stop.

The finger sealing the lips makes even the universally understood "shh . . ." quite unnecesssary; and different motions of the fingers can indicate "come," or "he is crazy" or something impolite or even obscene.

The unspoken vocabulary in fact is so extensive that two persons who do not understand each other's languages, can practically converse by communicating with only their hands and facial expressions.

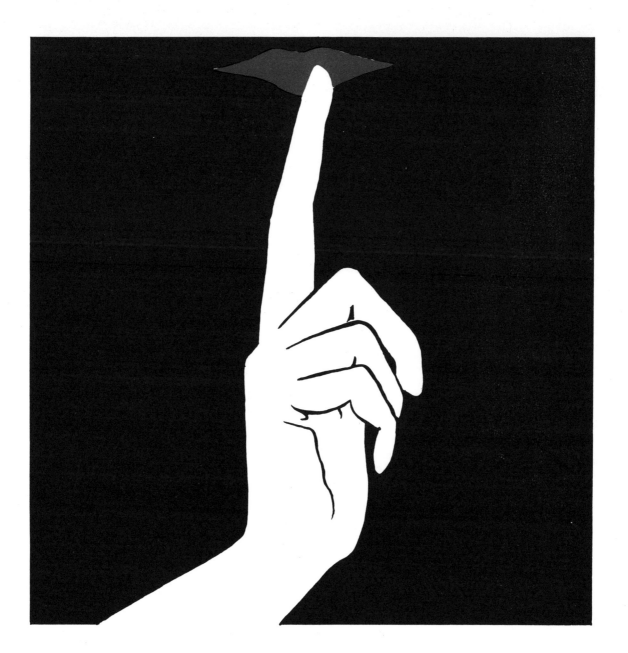

Deaf people must depend on visual communication. It is possible for many to "lip-read," that is to know what words a speaker is using by watching his lips.

But for speaking with each other, deaf-mutes use a manual alphabet, a system of finger positions, each of which represents a letter.

Forming words and sentences like this may seem to be a painstaking way of communicating, but it is surprising how efficient the system is once it becomes second nature, especially when shortcuts are used with the introduction of special agreed upon signs and symbols for words such as names of people and places.

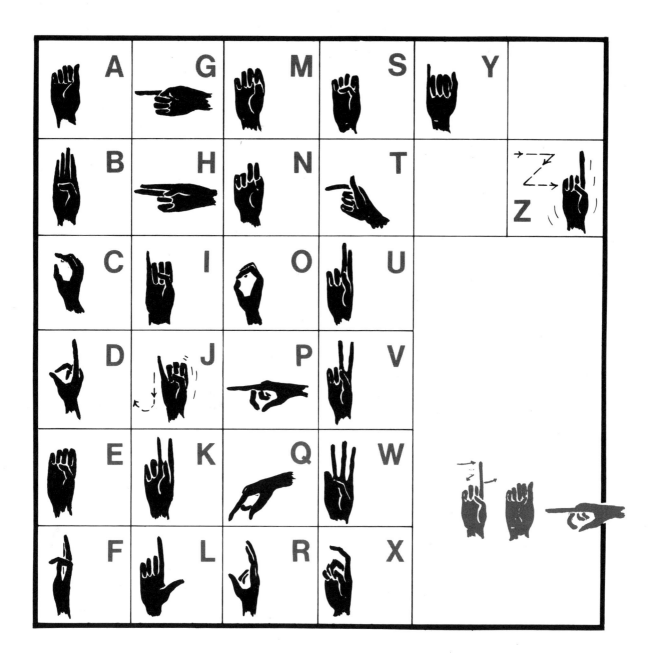

Raised dots on a page become symbols for letters to the blind who cannot see printed or written words. By running fingertips over the page, a blind person recognizes various combinations of dots and automatically translates them into words.

The system is called braille, after Louis Braille, a Frenchman who invented it in 1829.

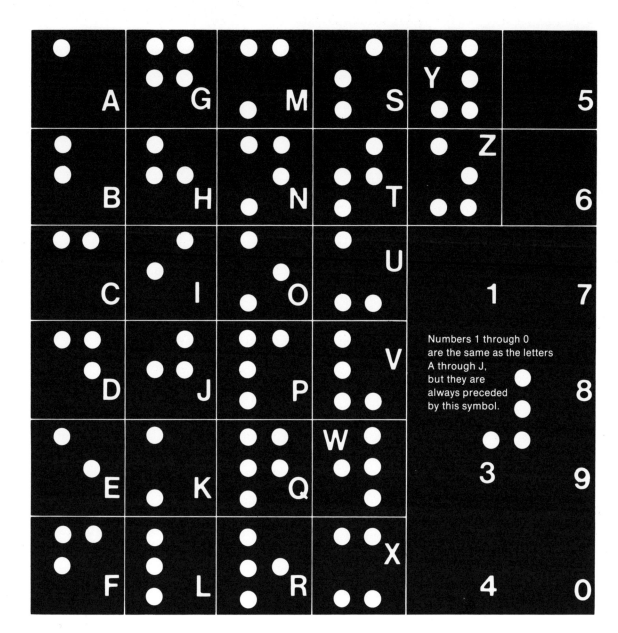

Numbers 1 through 0 are the same as the letters A through J, but they are always preceded by this symbol.

In the morse code, letters and numbers are represented by a system of dots and dashes, which can be translated into short and long beeps. These carried clearly by wire and wireless over long distances, in the days before voice communication was perfected. When ships were in viewing distance of the land or each other, they could also use the morse code by short and long flashes of light.

• • • – – – • • •   • • • – – – • • •   or

S O S S O S was the signal that ships used when in trouble. This has become the accepted symbol for the idea of "distress" and "send help."

Similarly, • • • – , the sign for V became synonymous with Victory when Winston Churchill, England's Prime Minister during the Second World War, greeted crowds by forming a V with his fingers. The sound • • • –   has become so ingrained in many of our minds that upon hearing the opening bars of Beethoven's Fifth Symphony, da da da DAAAAhhh, we assume something that was never intended.

Letter	Morse	Letter	Morse	Letter	Morse	Letter	Morse	Letter	Morse	Letter	Morse
A	·−	G	−−·	M	−−	S	···	Y	−·−−	5	····
B	−···	H	····	N	−·	T	−	Z	−−··	6	−····
C	−·−·	I	··	O	−−−	U	··−	1	·−−−−	7	−−···
D	−··	J	·−−−	P	·−−·	V	···−	2	··−−−	8	−−−··
E	·	K	−·−	Q	−−·−	W	·−−	3	···−−	9	−−−−·
F	··−·	L	·−··	R	·−·	X	−··−	4	····−	0	−−−−−

Semaphore was used by sailors for communicating between ships in the old days, when there were no radios or electric lights.

Semaphore is a system of signaling by the use of two flags, one held in each hand. The letters of the alphabet are represented by the various positions of the arms.

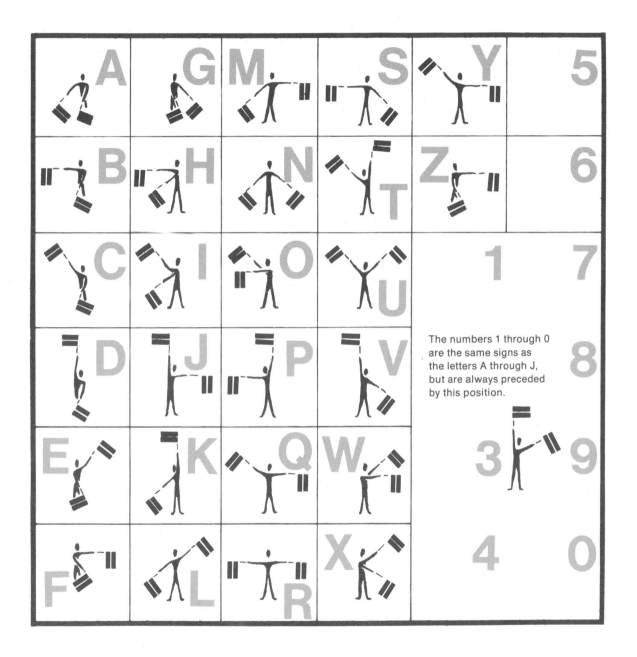

The numbers 1 through 0 are the same signs as the letters A through J, but are always preceded by this position.

Since pilots don't speak the languages of most of the countries in which they land their planes, an international "marshalling" system has been devised to get a plane in and out of its gate at the terminal.

With the use of easily seen paddles during the day, and electric light torches at night, the person on the ground goes through a series of motions, whose meanings the pilots understand, making it possible for them to follow the instructions given.

Musical symbols are known to almost everyone throughout the world. They are used by composers to record thoughts of sound, melody, rhythm and so on, on paper in such a way that others can recreate the sound, melody, rhythm and so on, exactly as they had been originally conceived.

The universal agreement on what these symbols mean makes it possible for any group of musicians to sing and play together by following the "music."

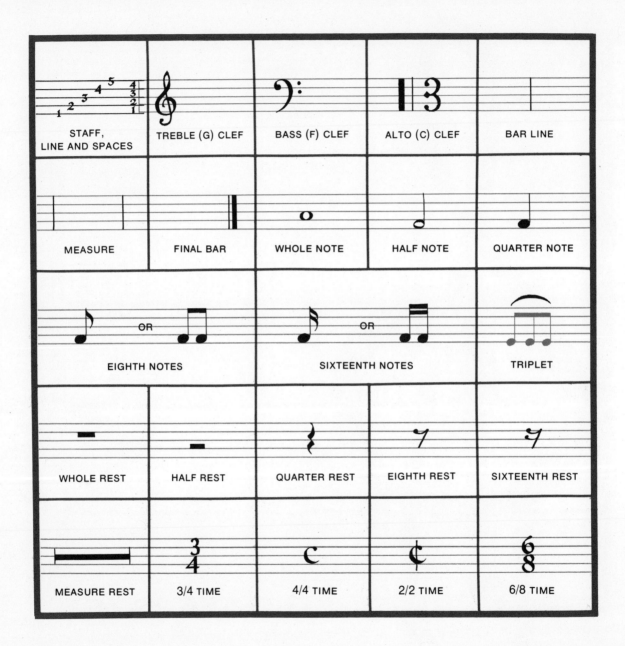

TRIAD	FERMATA	FLAT	DOUBLE FLAT	NATURAL
SHARP	DOUBLE SHARP	PIANO	PIANISSIMO	DISSONANCE
FORTE	FORTISSIMO	REPEAT	REPEAT ONE MEASURE	REPEAT FROM BEGINNING
REPEAT TWO MEASURES	TIE	SLUR	GLISSANDO	LEGATO
TRILL	STACCATO	CRESCENDO	DECRESCENDO	SWELL

Everything in the world—and probably in the universe—is structured from about one hundred basic chemicals known as elements. Some of these, such as gold, can be found in their pure state in nature, but most are locked in with other elements in different combinations. Together they form most of the solids, liquids and gasses that make up all the matter we know.

Na is the symbol chemists use for the metal sodium, and Cl the symbol for the gas chlorine. Combining one part of Na with one part of Cl the result becomes NaCl, which represents, and is, common everyday table salt.

Similarly, when two parts of the gas hydrogen (H) are combined with one part of the gas oxygen (O) the result is water, which chemically expressed is

$$H_2O.$$

With these symbols, scientists can describe the composition of most earthly things. Working with these symbols as tools has enabled them to create many of the things that are not found in nature, such as plastics and paints, strong metals and medicines, gasoline and glue.

ELEMENTS

Ac ACTINIUM	**Cl** CHLORINE	**Ho** HOLMIUM	**Np** NEPTUNIUM	**Se** SELENIUM
Ag SILVER	**Cm** CURIUM	**I** IODINE	**O** OXYGEN	**Si** SILICON
Al ALUMINUM	**Co** COBALT	**In** INDIUM	**Os** OSMIUM	**Sm** SAMARIUM
Am AMERICIUM	**Cr** CHROMIUM	**Ir** IRIDIUM	**P** PHOSPHORUS	**Sn** TIN
Ar ARGON	**Cs** CESIUM	**K** POTASSIUM	**Pa** PROTACTINIUM	**Sr** STRONTIUM
As ARSENIC	**Cu** COPPER	**Kr** KRYPTON	**Pb** LEAD	**Ta** TANTALUM
At ASTATINE	**Dy** DYSPROSIUM	**La** LANTHANUM	**Pd** PALLADIUM	**Tb** TERBIUM
Au GOLD	**Er** ERBIUM	**Li** LITHIUM	**Pm** PROMETHIUM	**Tc** TECHNETIUM
B BORON	**Es** EINSTEINIUM	**Lu** LUTETIUM	**Po** POLONIUM	**Te** TELLURIUM
Ba BARIUM	**Eu** EUROPIUM	**Lr** LAWRENCIUM	**Pr** PRASEODYMIUM	**Th** THORIUM
Be BERYLLIUM	**F** FLUORINE	**Md** MENDELEVIUM	**Pt** PLATINUM	**Ti** TITANIUM
Bi BISMUTH	**Fe** IRON	**Mg** MAGNESIUM	**Pu** PLUTONIUM	**Tl** THALLIUM
Bk BERKELIUM	**Fm** FERMIUM	**Mn** MANGANESE	**Ra** RADIUM	**Tm** THULIUM
Br BROMINE	**Fr** FRANCIUM	**Mo** MOLYBDENUM	**Rb** RUBIDIUM	**U** URANIUM
C CARBON	**Ga** GALLIUM	**N** NITROGEN	**Re** RHENIUM	**V** VANADIUM
Ca CALCIUM	**Gd** GADOLINIUM	**Na** SODIUM	**Rh** RHODIUM	**W** TUNGSTEN
Cd CADMIUM	**Ge** GERMANIUM	**Nb** NIOBIUM	**Rn** RADON	**Xe** XENON
Ce CERIUM	**H** HYDROGEN	**Nd** NEODYMIUM	**Ru** RUTHENIUM	**Y** YTTRIUM
Cf CALIFORNIUM	**He** HELIUM	**Ne** NEON	**S** SULFUR	**Yb** YTTERBIUM
	Hf HAFNIUM	**Ni** NICKEL	**Sb** ANTIMONY	**Zn** ZINC
	Hg MERCURY	**No** NOBELIUM	**Sc** SCANDIUM	**Zr** ZIRCONIUM

Na + Cl → NaCl

salt

Until a thousand years ago, the Western World used Roman letters instead of the numbers we know:

$$I = 1$$
$$V = 5$$
$$X = 10$$
$$L = 50$$
$$C = 100$$
$$D = 500$$
$$M = 1000$$

Other numbers were formed from these by adding or subtracting. The value of the symbol following another of the same or greater value is added:

III=3, VI=6, XVII=17, MDCCLXVIII=1768

The value of a symbol preceding another of the same or greater value is subtracted:

IX=9   XL=40   IC=99

The value of a symbol standing between two of greater value is subtracted from the second; the remainder being added to the value of the first:

XIX=19   MIC=1099   DXLIV=544

A bar over a letter indicates multiplication by 1000:

$\overline{V}$=5000 $\overline{CCC}$=300000

Let's remember to be grateful the next time we have to add up even something as simple as a grocery bill that we no longer use Roman numerals but something much less complicated.

MCMLXXIII

0 1 2 3 4 5 6 7 8 9

are among the most exciting and flexible symbols known to man. Each figure by itself stands for a very clear quantity. By combining these simple ten symbols, we can create countless variations.

Each can be added to, subtracted from, multiplied and divided by any other figure, which means that every number is bursting with infinite potential.

The symbols $+$, $-$, $\times$ and $\div$ are only some of the tools that allow us to release that energy for the use and enjoyment of the great world of numbers.

The mathematical symbols and their meaning are understood by all peoples on earth, regardless of cultural differences. In fact, if man is ever to meet a creature from outer space, the chances are that mathematical symbols will be the initial means of communication.

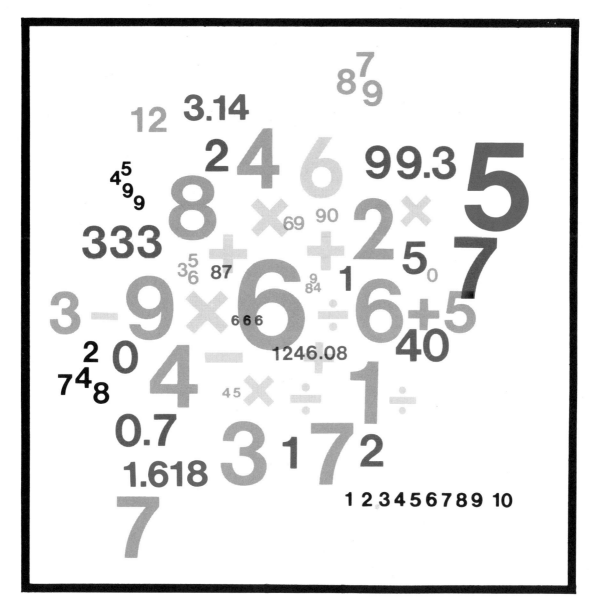

Infinity is the age of God—
        if you believe in Him;
        and if you don't,
Infinity is the time that Nature has been and will be after all the future that can
        be conceived.
Infinity is what is beyond the beyond in the sky, beyond the beyond that we can
        neither see nor imagine.
Infinity is endless and unlimited, without beginning and without end, so large or
        small that even numbers cannot express it. For this reason there is a
        special symbol that means infinity.

The origin of the symbol is probably derived from the Möbius strip, a surface with only one side, which can be formed by giving a half twist to a narrow, rectangular strip of paper and then pasting its two ends together. A line drawn on the center of the strip will be a line without beginning or end.

Astrology is the belief that the position of the sun in relationship to the stars and planets influences human affairs and behavior. The twelve signs of the zodiac symbolize the constellations or patterns of celestial bodies through which the sun and planets pass at specific times of each year.

Astrologers believe that each sign is associated with definite aspects of character, temperament, ability and physiology; and by establishing the relative positions of the stars at the date and hour of a person's birth, they claim the ability to predict his future and make recommendations on his course of action and behavior.

The signs of the zodiac go back to mythology, and abstract symbols for them have come down through the ages; representational images are used as well, in which Pisces (which means fish in Latin) is represented by two fish, scorpio by a scorpion, and so on.

Symbolism is part of game playing.

In chess for instance, each of the six basic pieces has a distinct design, and each is symbolic of specific powers and a prescribed set of movements. For example:

The ROOK is shaped like a castle tower and can
move in a vertical or horizontal direction.

The KNIGHT is shaped like a horse's head, and in a
single move is advanced one square in a vertical
or horizontal direction, and then one square diagonally.

A BISHOP is shaped like a bishop's miter with a slash in it,
and it moves in a diagonal direction across any
number of squares.

Chess players throughout the world know the meaning of these symbols, and they can play the game together without understanding each others' language, customs or cultures.

In card games, the heart, the spade, the diamond and the club are one set of symbols which are used in combination with a second set consisting of aces, numbers, jacks, queens and kings.

Sometimes these symbols assume different meanings, depending on how they are used. Their role and value will vary in the games of bridge, rummy, poker, pinochle or others, all of which are played with the same basic sets of cards.

Once the name of the game has been defined, each symbol becomes frozen into a precise role, and the game proceeds with each player understanding exactly the specific power and meaning of the symbols on the cards.

In some folklore the Ace of Spades meant DEATH.

When four men were in a lifeboat, for instance, that was designed to hold only three persons safely, it was obvious that one of them had to go. A deck of cards would be produced, the four aces removed for use, and after shuffling them, each man picked a card in turn.

The man who drew the Black Ace was thrown overboard to be eaten by the sharks.

There are many other such tales that "prove" the truth of the superstition.

The balanced scale that weighs evidence is the symbol for Justice.

Frequently, the scale is shown being held by a blindfolded female figure, symbolizing that she is completely objective and cannot be influenced by anything other than the weight of the evidence.

The figure is still shown draped in a toga, which indicates how little the concept has changed from the days of the Greeks and the Romans.

The related cliché that "Justice is blind" is in itself a symbolic statement whose meaning has been passed down from Biblical times.

Trademarks are symbols used to distinguish the products or services of a company from those of its competitors. Trademarks are usually registered with the government and protected by law so that no one else can use the same mark.

Sometimes the designs use a realistic image to convey the message. A little girl with an umbrella demonstrates that the salt the company produces will pour, even on days when it rains; a running greyhound identifies a bus company, and a topless fairy lass leaning over a brook may symbolize a sparkling soda water.

Sometimes, the name of the company itself becomes the trademark. Other times the design takes the form of letters or initials: VW can be interwoven into a symbol that everybody associates with a car, and NBC and BBC are related to broadcasting.

Other symbols are totally abstract, and familiarity with the design becomes a shorthand that requires no words to describe the company and what product or service it offers.

Aesculapius was a legendary Greek who is believed to have been the first professional doctor. In curing the sick, he used a great many secret medicines and methods; these included snakes. No one knows quite how he used them and just why, but apparently he was so successful that the Caduceus, which is Aesculapius' walking stick with a snake wound around it, has become the basic symbol for the profession of medicine.

Sometimes, for good measure, two snakes are used, and sometimes the Caduceus is shown with wings. That comes from one of the gods of ancient Greece, Hermes, the messenger of Zeus, the chief of all the gods. Hermes, who was called Mercury in Latin, carried a staff with wings on top, which presumably helped him get around more quickly.

It is all very confusing, but a fair guess is that doctors favor the design with wings on top of their Caduceus symbol, to remind everybody how helpfully and quickly they get to a patient's house when there is a call for help.

A candy-striped pole in front of a store symbolizes a barber shop; three balls hanging over the entrance means that there is a pawn broker doing business, and a wooden Indian in front of a shop once indicated the presence of a cigar store.

Until house numbers were introduced about two hundred years ago, practically all the shops were identified by merchant marks. Hanging over the street from the buildings were designs of fish, boots, pestles and mortars, gloves, lambs and other obvious symbols that described what was being sold.

Some of the signs were more subtle than others, and these were known as rebuses. A man whose name was T. Cox, for example might have had a sign over his door depicting three roosters, or a man called Percy Katz, may have had a sign showing two pussy cats.

As foreign travel increases, the United States Department of Transportation has recognized that a uniform standard of signage is necessary to help bridge the language barrier at airports, rail and bus terminals to identify different essential services. The American Institute of Graphic Arts was commissioned to create these Symbol Signs.

Are they self-explanatory?   Which is which?   Which are missing?

Taxi

Air Transportation

Toilets

Car rental

Ticket purchase

No Smoking

No entry

Mail   Bus

Baggage Lockers   Information

Restaurant

Bar   Coffee shop   Lost and Found

Telephone

First Aid

Hotel Information   Elevator

No parking

There are many symbols that identify people, what they do, who they are and where they come from.

A wedding ring indicates that a person is married. A graduation ring shows what school a person attended; and a pendant with a star of David shows that a person is Jewish.

If the license plate on a car indicates a DPL, chances are the car belongs to a diplomat. If the plates have an MD on them, it means that the owner is a doctor. And if the number on the plate is "1," it is the car of the governor of the state.

A cockney accent, a Texas drawl or a Caribbean singsong identifies a person's place of origin; a person's manners, use of language, clothes, all become symbols of background, education and taste.

When they are all wearing bathing suits it is not possible to tell who is a waiter, a priest, a policeman or a circus clown. When they are in their working clothes, it takes only a glance to recognize who is who.

Soldiers, sailors and marines are known by their uniforms. Insignia and patches on those uniforms are symbols of rank, organizations, and specific jobs; ribbons tell in what wars their owners fought, if they were wounded and what medals they have earned.

The term "coat of arms" stems from the times when knights in battle wore protective armor from head to foot, making it impossible for them to be recognized by friend or foe. The knights solved this problem by wearing a light cloth "coat" over their armor, which was decorated with an identifying personal design.

Since eventually a coat of arms became an important status symbol, practically every important family, town and even institution adopted one. To avoid total confusion, a common design language had to be established if the designs were to have meaning to anyone other than the owners.

For this reason, the science of heraldry was devised. A heraldic "college" was established, a type of committee appointed by the king. The college set rules and standards for who could have a coat of arms, what materials they were made of, how the shield was to be divided, and what the crest symbolized. The college defined the meaning of each animal, plant or abstract design, the modifications required as the coat of arms was passed on from one generation to the next, the means by which special achievements and honors were to be represented and so on, to such a detailed degree, that there are more than eight hundred special heraldic terms in the English language alone that describe the meaning of these symbols.

To those who understand the heraldic symbolism of the crests and shields in their infinite variations, the designs make for exciting historical gossip. For the rest of us, however, the coats of arms must remain just colorful but meaningless designs.

Just plain sounds can be symbols—non-verbal shortcuts to a whole world of communication, understood by all.

Shhhhh . . . means *quiet!!*   *OUCH!!!!*   means it hurts.

Sighhhhhh can be a form of desperation, but a different sounding sigh can mean relief.

Pst! Pst! will draw someone's attention, but *ps-ps-ps* will call a cat to dinner.

TS TS TS will make some horses go faster, and a clicking sound *CL CL CL* will do the same thing for others.

Yet a single, emphatic TS! means NO to any Greek, (especially if the head is thrown back at the same time). A whistle of a certain type expresses admiration for a girl; a whistle of another type may stand for amazement or surprise, while a third type of whistle, in some societies, may be used instead of *BOOOOO*. . . .

A door can be SLAMMED, a desk can be BANGED, and WHAM!!

The world knows someone is angry.

WOW

WOW

WHAM

ZAP

Words themselves are symbols. If we want to describe an animal that has four legs, is furry and is a domesticated mammal that barks, we simply use the word DOG, and we all know the idea is "dogness."

If we want to describe an animal that has four legs, is furry and is a domesticated mammal that purrs, we use the word CAT, and we all get the idea of "catness"

To communicate that idea we now simply write "dog" or "cat."

But it wasn't always as easy . . .

One of the earliest forms of writing was hieroglyphics, which means "holy carving." The name was given to the writing of the ancient Egyptians because much of the earliest writing studied was carved into the stone work of temples and tombs. The name still applies, even though a great deal of early Egyptian writing that exists is painted on walls, on papyrus and wood, carved into ivory and cast or hammered onto gold.

Hieroglyphics is a system of symbols in which words and phrases were formed by combining basic characters, some symbolizing specific objects or concepts with others representing spoken sounds.

Some examples of the first type:

fish		water		fire, to cook, burn		strength	
rain, storm		house		smell (good or bad)		to walk, stand, and of actions	
day, time		to cut, slay		to overthrow		children	

To illustrate the typical "sound" type character, the word for "mouth" was represented by this obvious symbol ⬯, which was pronounced "RA." The symbol is used for the letter "R." Sound symbols were especially useful in writing proper names, for which there could be no visual representation. Other examples include:

A		F		S	
or I		or M		SH	
or U		or N		K	
B		H		Q	

EXTRACT FROM TALE OF TWO BROTHERS

His brother elder
became like panthers southern. He
made sharp his dagger,
he placed it in his hand.
His brother elder stood
behind the door of his
stable to stab his
brother younger at his coming at
eventide to make enter his
cattle into the stables.

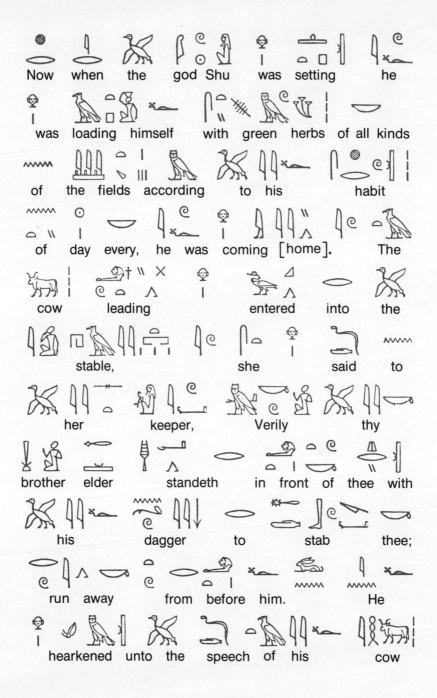

Now when the god Shu was setting he was loading himself with green herbs of all kinds of the fields according to his habit of day every, he was coming [home]. The cow leading entered into the stable, she said to her keeper, Verily thy brother elder standeth in front of thee with his dagger to stab thee; run away from before him. He hearkened unto the speech of his cow

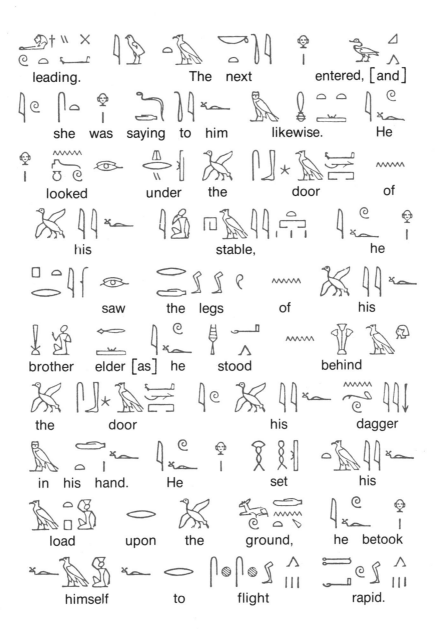

leading. The next entered, [and]
she was saying to him likewise. He
looked under the door of
his stable, he
saw the legs of his
brother elder [as] he stood behind
the door his dagger
in his hand. He set his
load upon the ground, he betook
himself to flight rapid.

Chinese writing, forms of which are also used by the Japanese and the Koreans, started out originally as representational images, symbols for recognizable things that conveyed ideas. Over many millenia, these images developed into the characters used today, and in some of them, the origin is still evident.

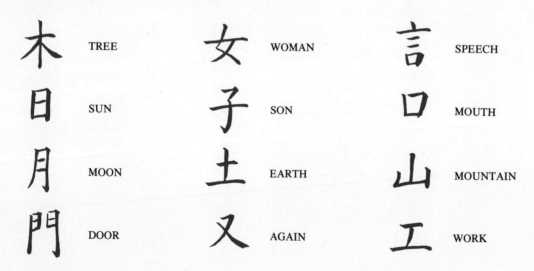

Even though there are some 40,000 character combinations in the Chinese vocabulary—about 1800 are needed for reading a newspaper—this is not as complicated as it seems, since there are relatively few characters that appear in most words. These are the "simple" characters.

木	TREE	女	WOMAN	言	SPEECH
日	SUN	子	SON	口	MOUTH
月	MOON	土	EARTH	山	MOUNTAIN
門	DOOR	又	AGAIN	工	WORK

To form other words, compound characters are created by putting together two or more simple characters. One way of doing this is to create a ''logical'' compound, where two characters (or elements) suggest similar qualities:

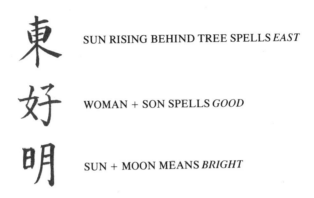

SUN RISING BEHIND TREE SPELLS *EAST*

WOMAN + SON SPELLS *GOOD*

SUN + MOON MEANS *BRIGHT*

Another way of building a compound character, is to create a ''phonetic'' compound, where one element indicates the sense of the word, and the other suggests the original sound of the word. In Chinese, many of the words sound the same but have a different meaning.

''FANG'' MAY MEAN *A PLACE, METHOD, WAY, REGION SQUARE,* OR MAY BE A SURNAME

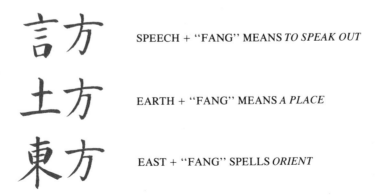

SPEECH + ''FANG'' MEANS *TO SPEAK OUT*

EARTH + ''FANG'' MEANS *A PLACE*

EAST + ''FANG'' SPELLS *ORIENT*

Think of the letters of the alphabet as characters which either alone or in combination with other letters become symbolic of the sounds which create the spoken words. Letters are also shortcuts. When reading what is written, the mind can register at a glance the meaning, not only of the single words themselves, but even phrases and sometimes whole sentences—bypassing entirely the impression of and the need for the sounds that letters represent.

The wonder of it is that with only twenty-six basic letters, combinations of words can be formed to express and record practically everything that man has experienced on every level.

The punctuation marks form a supporting sub-system of symbols which enrich and clarify the communication between the writer and his reader.

HENRY ADAMS   JOHN ADDISON   AESCHYLUS   AESOP   LOUISA MAY ALCOTT
HANS CHRISTIAN ANDERSEN   MAXWELL ANDERSON   SHERWOOD ANDERSON
JEAN ANOUILH   THOMAS AQUINAS   ARISTOPHANES   ARISTOTLE   MATTHEW
ARNOLD   SHOLEM ASH   W.H. AUDEN   SAINT ANTHONY   JANE AUSTEN
SIR FRANCIS BACON   HONORE DE BALZAC   VICKI BAUM   SAMUEL BECKET
MAX BEERBOHM   EDWARD BELLAMY   STEPHEN VINCENT BENNETT   AMBROSE
BIERCE   WILLIAM BLAKE   JAMES BOSWELL   ELIZABETH BOWDEN   BERTOLT
BRECHT   ANNE BRONTE   ROBERT BROWNING   WILLIAM CULLEN BRYANT
ROBERT BURNS   SAMUEL BUTLER   JULIUS CAESAR   ERSKINE CALDWELL
ALBERT CAMUS   THOMAS CARLYLE   LEWIS CARROLL   JOYCE CARY   WILLA
CATHER   CERVANTES   GEOFFREY CHAUCER   ANTON CHEKHOV   WINSTON
CHURCHILL   JEAN COCTEAU   SAMUEL TAYLOR COLERIDGE   CONFUCIUS
WILLIAM CONGREVE   JOSEPH CONRAD   JAMES FENIMORE COOPER   NOEL
COWARD   CHARLES DARWIN   DANTE   CHARLES DICKENS   EMILY DICKINSON
ISAK DINESEN   JOHN DONNE   JOHN DOS PASSOS   DOSTOEVSKI   ARTHUR CONAN
DOYLE   THEODORE DREISER   DUMAS   GEORGE ELIOT   T.S. ELIOT   RALPH WALDO
EMERSON   EURIPIDES   WILLIAM FAULKNER   F. SCOTT FITZGERALD   FLAUBERT
SHAKESPEARE   C.S. FORESTER   E.M. FORSTER   BENJAMIN FRANKLIN   ROBERT
FROST   GOETHE   GARCIA LORCA   OLIVER GOLDSMITH   ROBERT GRAVES
GRAHAM GREENE   GORKY   THOMAS HARDY   HEINRICH HEINE   ERNEST HEMINGWAY
O. HENRY   HERODOTUS   ROBERT HERRICK   JOHN HERSEY   THOMAS HEYWOOD
HOMER   VICTOR HUGO   DAVID HUME   ALDOUS HUXLEY   HENRIK IBSEN   WASHINGTON
IRVING   HENRY JAMES   ROBINSON JEFFERS   THOMAS JEFFERSON   JAMES JOYCE
FRANZ KAFKA   E.J. KAHN   IMMANUEL KANT   JOHN KEATS   KIERKEGAARD   RUDYARD KIPLING
ARTHUR KOESTLER   D.H. LAWRENCE   T.E. LAWRENCE   SINCLAIR LEWIS
JOHN LOCKE   HENRY WADSWORTH LONGFELLOW   LUCRETIUS   ARCHIBALD MacLEISH
MACHIAVELLI   ANDRE MALRAUX   THOMAS MANN   KARL MARX   SOMERSET MAUGHAM
GUY DE MAUPASSANT   HERMAN MELVILLE   H.L. MENCKEN   GEORGE MEREDITH
EDNA ST. VINCENT MILLAY   JOHN MILTON   MOLIERE   THOMAS MOORE   SIR ISAAC
NEWTON   NIETZSCHE   SEAN O'CASEY   JOHN O'HARA   EUGENE O'NEILL   JOSE
ORTEGA Y GASSET   GEORGE ORWELL   THOMAS PAINE   SAMUEL PEPYS   PETRONIUS
PINDAR   PLATO   PLUTARCH   EDGAR ALLAN POE   MARCO POLO   ALEXANDER POPE
EZRA POUND   MARCEL PROUST   ALEXANDER PUSHKIN   RABELAIS   RACINE   RILKE
RIMBAUD   ROUSSEAU   CARL SANDBURG   GEORGE SAND   GEORGE SANTAYANA   WILLIAM
SAROYAN   SARTRE   SCHILLER   SCHOPENHAUER   SIR WALTER SCOTT   WILLIAM
SHAKESPEARE   GEORGE BERNARD SHAW   SHELLEY   ROBERT SHERWOOD   UPTON SINCLAIR
ISRAEL SINGER   SOPHOCLES   SPINOZA   JOHN STEINBECK   STENDHAL   ROBERT LOUIS
STEVENSON   TACITUS   BOOTH TARKINGTON   ALFRED TENNYSON   DYLAN THOMAS
THOREAU   JAMES THURBER   TOLSTOY   ARNOLD TOYNBEE   MARK TWAIN   JULES VERNE
VOLTAIRE   EVELYN WAUGH   H.G. WELLS   EDITH WHARTON   WALT WHITMAN   OSCAR
WILDE   TENNESSEE WILLIAMS   WILLIAM CARLOS WILLIAMS   THOMAS WOLFE   VIRGINIA
WOOLF   WILLIAM WADSWORTH   XENOPHON   WILLIAM BUTLER   YEATS   EMILE ZOLA

Symbols, symbols everywhere.

Elephants for Republicans.
Donkeys for Democrats.
Blue for boy, and pink for girl.
Red for stop, and green for go.
Soft music, candlelight, sweet smell of good perfume—
　　romance and love.

The sounds of jingle bells or the sight of a decorated evergreen tree for Christmas.

　　The trumpet sound of taps, for mourning. RSVP and POB, USSR and COD, abbreviations, symbols, understood by people in many countries. There is the @ and #, the % and &,%, Co., and Inc. which is Ltd. in the UK.
Etc. etc. etc.
　　Even names are symbols, representing specific people, and sometimes the ideas they have expressed.

A symbol is a shortcut as long as someone else can understand its meaning.

Over & out, as the pilots say when they mean

The End

●